BE THE PERSON

YOUR DOG

THINKS YOU ARE

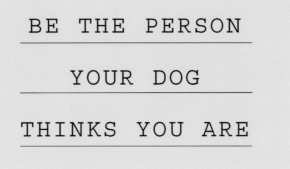

BE THE PERSON

YOUR DOG

THINKS YOU ARE

C. J. Frick

Drawings by Liza Donnelly

FLATIRON
BOOKS
NEW YORK

www.flatironbooks.com

Illustrations by Liza Donnelly

Designed by Steven Seighman

The Library of Congress Cataloging-in-Publication Data is available upon request.

ISBN 978-1-250-17969-2 (paper over board)
ISBN 978-1-250-17970-8 (ebook)

Our books may be purchased in bulk for promotional, educational, or business use. Please contact your local bookseller or the Macmillan Corporate and Premium Sales Department at 1-800-221-7945, extension 5442, or by email at MacmillanSpecialMarkets@macmillan.com.

First Edition: October 2018

10   9   8   7   6   5   4   3   2   1

To Oliver, who made me a better human every day

—LIZA DONNELLY

For Wally, the best dog there ever was

—C. J. FRICK

BE THE PERSON

YOUR DOG

THINKS YOU ARE

To be the person your dog thinks you are, you should...

Be affectionate.

Prepare for the worst.

Be willing to burn the midnight oil.

Be wise enough to
walk away from conflict.

Get your hands dirty.

Be a team player.

make time for what's
really important.

Appreciate the little things.

Be generous.

Be spontaneous.

Be determined.

sit. —

Teach with patience.

Celebrate special occasions.

Exercise regularly.

Know when to break the rules.

Be brave.

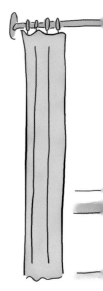

Appreciate the sacrifices of others.

Embrace the open road.

make new friends.

Be encouraging.

Be thankful for downtime.

Be the best part
of someone's day.

Be a friend for all seasons.

Forgive freely.

Protect the (adorably) fearful.

Respect routine.

Love nature.

Be part of your community.

Be charitable.

Be patient.

Expect the unexpected.

keep an open mind.

Take the time to
make someone smile.

Lead with courage.

Be good in bed.

Be able to let loose.

understand that life
comes with messes.

Be gentle.

Be tough when required.

Embrace a lifelong commitment.

Be the person your dog
thinks you are.

ACKNOWLEDGMENTS

Thanks to Michael.

—LIZA DONNELLY

Thanks to the team at Flatiron Books, past and present,
for being almost as wonderful as a dog.

—C. J. FRICK